www.kaynorth.com

Email: info@kaynorth.com

Dedicated to you...yes YOU!

"Success comes when preparation meets opportunity."

Congratulations on taking this step to prepare!

Table of Contents

Written permission to reprint any contents of this workbook must be requested at info@kaynorth.com

Who is **K**ay North?

I am a veteran of the US Navy, supply chain analyst, start-up entrepreneur, and career strategist. As a professional goal and career alignment strategist, I am known for my ability to visualize the big picture and zoom in on the smaller pieces to make dreams come true. I will enable you to create and re-invent yourself to produce results that add quality and value to life through an ideal career path.

In 2008, I took on the challenge of transitioning from logistics to recruiting, and I discovered my passion of motivating and mentoring people as they sought out a journey to success.

Introducing new options that lead to progress and transformation is a tremendous factor in obtaining quality of life. I delight in coaching individuals to align goals with a strategy, overcome challenges, and live life with purpose.

I teach the following workshops: The Nature of Being an Entrepreneur, Career Strategy & Goal Alignment, Resumes, Interview Skills, Time Management, Mind-set, and Dress for Success, to name a few.

As a lifelong learner and dedicated coach, I attend workshops and seminars provided by Alabama Small Business Development Center and network with other seasoned professionals. I am a member of the Opelika Chamber of Commerce, Disabled American Veterans, and have a partnership agreement with Goodwill Southern Rivers.

I received a Master of Science in Acquisition and Supply Chain Management from University of Maryland. I graduated with a Bachelor of Science in Business Operations Management from Excelsior College in Albany, NY. I completed 4000 hours of extensive training in the field of Life and Career Coaching by the Department of Labor.

Raised in a small city and having traveled the world, I was given the opportunity to experience different cultures and gain the required knowledge needed to succeed. I look forward to depositing my knowledge and experiences into aspiring individuals.

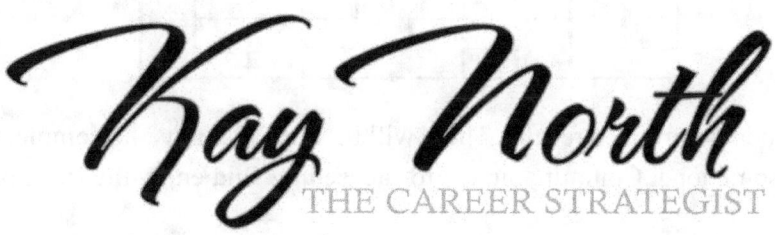

THE CAREER STRATEGIST

I build. I develop. I produce results.

Why Use this Model?

So, you ask, why should I read this book and use Kay North's model?

Because it works. Period. If you use this workbook and model as intended, you will become aware of your dreams, thoughts, career options, goals, strengths, and weaknesses. You will gain more clarity, a sense of direction, and motivation for your future. You will be provided with a personalized action plan to map your course to career and life success. This book is broken down into three parts: Career Strategy, Basic Entrepreneurship, and Necessary Internal and External Changes. Although one section may not be of use to you right now, it can be helpful to read it as it may give you additional inspiration.

In short, life looks like this: God created us with the ability to do great things and overcome all challenging obstacles. However, we are not born with a map or hand held guide to direct us in utilizing our abilities to be successful. Some people are born in undesirable circumstances- maybe to a poor family, an alcoholic mother or father, an abusive family member, raised by our grandparents- with no example of success. Overcoming the challenges of our environment is a key factor in career and life fulfillment.

The challenges of our environment are mere obstacles that we must go through to get to a life of success or our destiny. Think of a maze on a video game. When the character enters into the maze, it appears to be a smooth route, only to be confronted with dead ends, road blocks, and possibly enemies to defeat before advancing further. While inside the maze, the character doesn't know the distance to the end of the maze. He or she must simply keep going. Now replace the video maze with our environment. You may have been born into an undesirable maze, but the key to overcoming is to keep going. Do not get stuck, settle at a dead-end wall, and become a product of your environment.

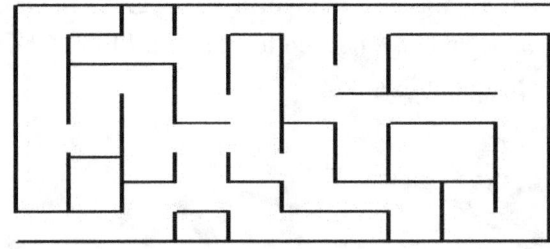

I created this model to produce results. There will be work that must be completed, some easy, some hard, some quick, and some long. Commit yourself to succeeding, and enjoy the fruits of your labor!

PART I:
Career Strategy

Self Assessments

Career Exploration

Goals—Understanding Your Why

Individual Development Action Plan

Resumes

Understanding Part I: Career Strategy

Part one of this workbook is for those of you who are interested in developing or furthering your career, but are unsure of how to implement a systematic approach to obtain your desired results. I created this program to enable you to identify career fields that match your personality; research qualification, requirements, and growth outlook; align goals and establish your why; and create a personalized action plan to identify and change existing behaviors that have prevented you from moving forward.

Career Strategy is divided into four elements: Understanding Self-Assessments, Conducting Career Exploration, Goals & Understanding Your Why, and Creating an Individual Development Action Plan. The following sections have interactive worksheets for your personalization: Conducting Career Exploration, Goals & Understanding Your Why, and Creating an Individual Development Action Plan. Each worksheet includes a recommended completion time. It is important for you to adhere to my recommendation for the comprehension of your research. The overall program should take you four weeks to complete. You must identify an accountability partner prior to creating your Individual Development Action Plan.

After you have completed your IDAP, review the Resume section, which is an important aspect in each stage of career development. You will find informative charts, sample resume templates, a list of action verbs, and a resume planning worksheet.

Read each section thoroughly. Let's begin!

Element I:
Understanding Self-Assessments

What is self-assessment? It is looking at your progress, development, and learning to determine what has improved and what areas need improvement. Career-seekers and career changers need to increase self-awareness in order to identify educational and career options best suited to them. Your personality, interests, values, and skills play an important role in your career choice. Let's take a look into each area.

Personality

Your personality is the makeup of who you are. It comprises of your energy level, flexibility, organization, and communication style. Your personality plays a major role in how you respond to the world around you. It can affect how enjoyable you find certain activities, whether it be parachuting, building a comprehensive collection of coins or performing complex calculations. It is hardly surprising then that understanding your personality type, and taking it into consideration when looking at career opportunities can influence how enjoyable you might find a particular role or career, (Researchskills.com). There are several free personality tests online that can identify your personality type.

Interests

Your interests and experiences start from the moment you participate in childhood activities. Reflecting on all of the activities you have participated in during the last five years, including school, work, volunteering, and leisure, will help you gain insight on your pattern of interests. Ask yourself the following questions and look for themes or patterns (e.g. a preference for activities that involve working with your hands):

- What have you liked and disliked about each activity?

- What did you learn from each activity?

- Which (if any) aspects of the activity would you like to remain involved with?

Values

Values are beliefs we develop early in life that make up our fundamental beliefs about what is right and wrong, good and bad. They are shaped by our family, culture, education, religion, and different socialization processes. Some values are maintained throughout our lives, while others may change and become more or less important over time. There are countless values, including having a family, having financial stability, being healthy, following our religious beliefs, having job security, etc. Take the time to consider and list what is most important to you. Once you have listed your values, identify:

- Values that you must have at work,

- Values that you would like to have at work, but are not necessary, and

- Values that are least important to you.

Skills

There are two types of skills: hard skills and soft skills. Hard skills are easily measured and consist of factual knowledge that is usually learned during formal training or at school. Hard skills include technical expertise, laboratory techniques, computer skills, and languages. Whereas soft skills (or transferable skills) are somewhat less tangible and can be acquired in various areas of one's life, such as school, work, or extra-curricular activities. These skills, which include your interpersonal and communication capabilities can be transferred to various work situations, (McGill).

Completing a self-assessment may also help you discover more career options available for you according to results based on each area described. The internet contains several free self-assessment tests. To take an accurate self-assessment, visit www.kaynorth.com, and click on the Career Assessment icon.

Notes

Element II:
Career Exploration and Planning

     Career planning is not an activity that should be done once—in high school or college—and left behind as we move forward in our jobs and careers. Career planning is an activity that is best done on a regular basis—especially given the data that the average worker will change careers multiple times over his or her lifetime.

     Creating a career plan forces you to take stock of your existing education, credentials, talents, and aspirations, which can help you draft an effective course of action that will put you on the path to career and life fulfillment. Whether you know your ideal career path or are unsure, my Career Exploration Worksheet will help you find useful information to help you focus and give you direction.

     On pages 14 and 15, you will see the Career Exploration Worksheet. The goal of the worksheet is to teach you how to research and analyze your career options, assess any additional qualifications or skills needed, and choose the career option that you'd like to begin first. The Career Exploration Worksheet is the beginning stage of your research. As you dive into each section, you will find that you may need to perform further research, such as types of credentials and colleges or universities who offer a program that correspond to your ideal career path.

     If you are undecided on a specific career, the worksheet provides you space to research three option, and you can use the notes section for other searches. If you are like myself and have an array of career ideas, narrow your options down to what you think you can accomplish within the next five years, and then choose your top choice. To complete your worksheet, visit www.kaynorth.com, and click on the icon labeled "My Next Move".

     This is a good place to introduce you to a coaching timeline. I set my clients on a reasonable timeline to get each stage our coaching sessions completed and to allow fresh information to soak in. You'll want to allow yourself the recommended time to complete each assignment before moving on. I have included a built-in calendar for your use. "Thank you Kay." You're welcome! :)

Timeframe to complete the Career Exploration Worksheet: 1 week

Month:

Sun	Mon	Tue	Wed	Thu	Fri	Sat

Month:

Sun	Mon	Tue	Wed	Thu	Fri	Sat

	EXAMPLE	Career Option
Job Title:	Supply Chain Manager	
Main Duties:	Purchases materials, tracks shipment, negotiates contracts and prices, improves supply chain	
Qualifications What are they? Do you have them? How easily can you get them?	--High school diploma/GED; Bachelor's degree in Business; Master's degree in Acquisition and Supply Chain Management; Optional certification	
Abilities and Skills What are they? Do you have them? Can you develop them?	Critical thinking, problem solving, multi-tasking, negotiating, attention to detail, communication (verbal and written), computer savvy, organized	
Work Roles & Work Styles? Which interest areas may you express in this career?	Most work in offices, warehouses, and may travel a lot meeting suppliers. Must be ethical according to US standards and foreign standards.	
Values & Personal Preferences How does this career compare to your values? Does it require you to do things you would prefer not to do?	I'd prefer to work smarter rather than harder. This career field allows me to improve processes. I love to travel, and negotiate contracts. I'd prefer safety and standards over cutting corners for money	
Work Environment Physical environment of work? Climate or culture of the organization(s) in which you might work?	Possible lifting of boxes up to 50 lbs. Use of warehouse equipment and office equipment Must be team player, be able to collaborate with other departments, and able to work independently	
Demands on the Worker Physical demands? Mental demands? Emotional demands?	Physical demands are traveling, some lifting. Mental demands are improving processes such as shipment, negotiating prices and contracts;	
$$Pay & Benefits Wage, salary, commission, etc.? Starting pay estimates (high & low)? Average income? Highest income possible? Benefits? Employment Outlook—growth or decline?	--Pay varies according to location and company. Highest pay is $100,000+ , lowest is +/- $60,000. Most positions offer benefits and retirement. Growth potential and job security is expected. However, competition is increasing as more companies outsource supply chain functions.	

	Career Option	Career Option
Job Title:		
Main Duties:		
Qualifications What are they? Do you have them? How easily can you get them?		
Abilities and Skills What are they? Do you have them? Can you develop them?		
Work Roles & Work Styles? Which interest areas may you express in this career?		
Values & Personal Preferences How does this career compare to your values? Does it require you to do things you would prefer not to do?		
Work Environment Physical environment of work? Climate or culture of the organization(s) in which you might work?		
Demands on the Worker Physical demands? Mental demands? Emotional demands?		
$$Pay & Benefits Wage, salary, commission, etc.? Starting pay estimates (high & low)? Average income? Highest income possible? Benefits? Employment Outlook—growth or decline?		

Notes

Element III:
Goals and Goal Alignment

To plan your career, first create the "big picture" of what you want to do with your life, and identify large scale goals you want to achieve. Once your large goals are identified, you must break those down into smaller SMART goals. We'll explore SMART goals further below, but first, let's identify why goal setting is important:

- Goals propel you forward.
- Goals transform overwhelming mountains into walkable hills.
- Goals help us believe in ourselves.
- Goals hold us accountable for failure.
- Goals tell us what we truly want.
- Goals help us live life to the fullest.

Your goals should be specific, measureable, attainable or achievable, realistic and relevant, and have a timeline. Review the table below that explains the characteristics of SMART goals.

S	**Specific:** State exactly what you want to accomplish (Who, What, Where, Why)
M	**Measurable:** How will you demonstrate and evaluate the extent to which the goal has been met?
A	**Achievable:** Make sure your goal is not too far to reach, but far enough to be challenging.
R	**Relevant:** How does the goal tie into your key responsibilities? How is it aligned to objectives?
T	**Time-bound:** Set one or more target dates, the "by when" to guide your goal to successful and timely completion (include deadlines, dates, and frequency)

By now you should have completed your career exploration worksheet, and selected one career option that you want to begin working on. As explained in the SMART goals table, your goals must be realistic and relevant. In this case, you must identify goals that are relevant to your selected career option. For example, let's pretend that your selected career option is auto mechanic, and you are a junior in high school. Your first relevant goal should be to graduate with your high school diploma. Your second relevant goal should be to enroll in a college or trade school that offers a certification for auto mechanics. A third relevant goal could be to graduate from the certification program. The fourth relevant goal could be to obtain employment working in your field to gain experience. After achieving those goals, you will position yourself to go higher in the mechanic world, such as managing a team of mechanics or owning a mechanic shop.

On pages 19 and 20, you will find a completed Goals—Understanding the Why worksheet for you to use as a guide, and then a blank worksheet for your completion. This worksheet serves two purposes: to establish goals from your career exploration and to plant seeds of "why" in your being. The effect of your "why" will come in handy as you travel on your journey to career/life fulfillment. The people who quit before they succeed do so because they never established their why or neglected to return to their "why".

Timeframe to complete the Goals & Understanding Your Why Worksheet: 1 week

SAMPLE—Goals & Understanding Your WHY

Whether we achieve our goals depends on whether we take action. But what decides whether we take action in the first place? How motivated you are! So, simply pick your top 3 goals, then answer the questions below. Keep writing even if you repeat your answers. The information below will help you feel clear, focused, and more motivated to achieve your goals.

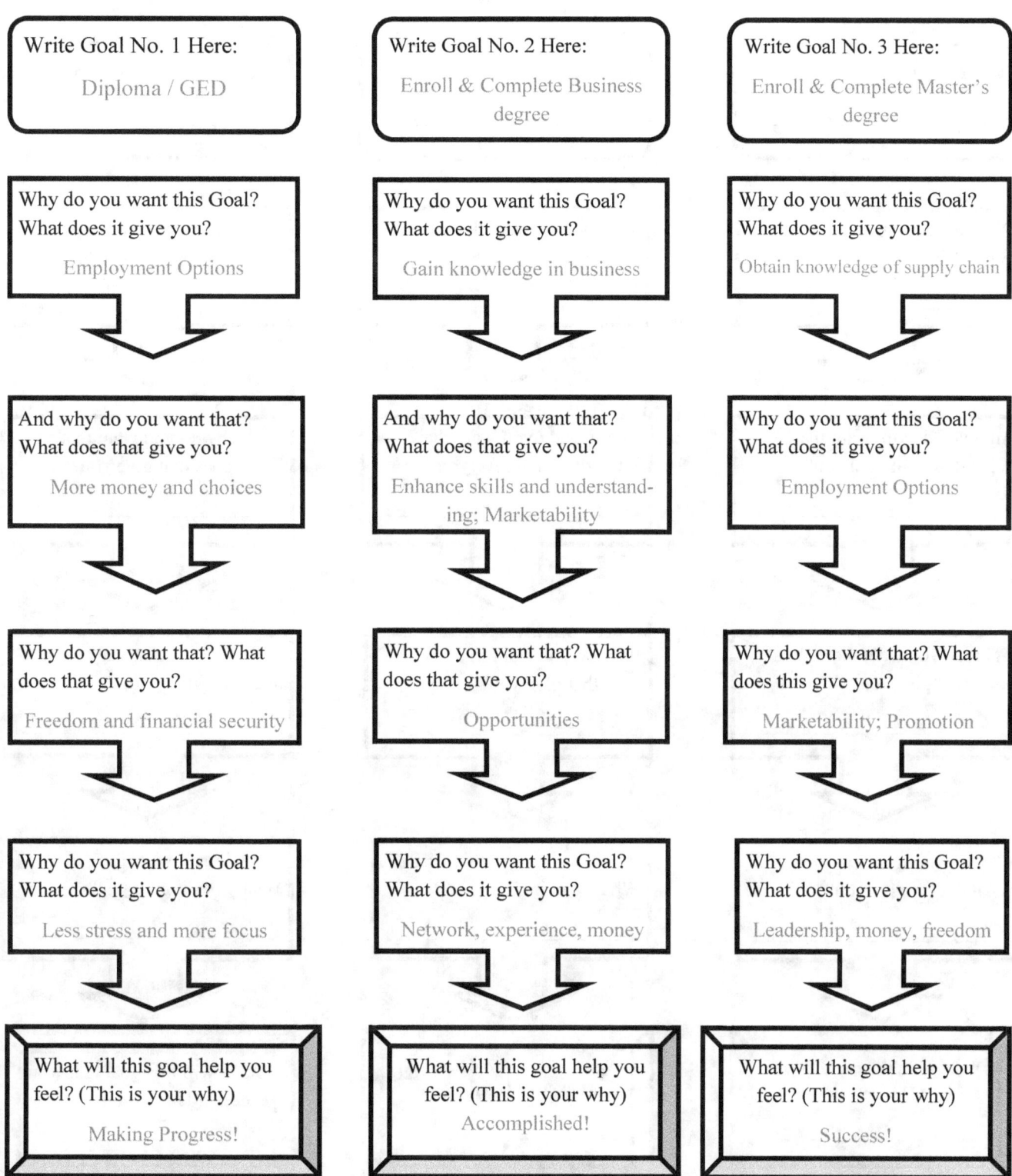

Write Goal No. 1 Here:

Diploma / GED

Write Goal No. 2 Here:

Enroll & Complete Business degree

Write Goal No. 3 Here:

Enroll & Complete Master's degree

Why do you want this Goal? What does it give you?

Employment Options

Why do you want this Goal? What does it give you?

Gain knowledge in business

Why do you want this Goal? What does it give you?

Obtain knowledge of supply chain

And why do you want that? What does that give you?

More money and choices

And why do you want that? What does that give you?

Enhance skills and understanding; Marketability

Why do you want this Goal? What does it give you?

Employment Options

Why do you want that? What does that give you?

Freedom and financial security

Why do you want that? What does that give you?

Opportunities

Why do you want that? What does this give you?

Marketability; Promotion

Why do you want this Goal? What does it give you?

Less stress and more focus

Why do you want this Goal? What does it give you?

Network, experience, money

Why do you want this Goal? What does it give you?

Leadership, money, freedom

What will this goal help you feel? (This is your why)

Making Progress!

What will this goal help you feel? (This is your why)

Accomplished!

What will this goal help you feel? (This is your why)

Success!

Goals & Understanding Your WHY

Whether we achieve our goals depends on whether we take action. But what decides whether we take action in the first place? How motivated you are! So, simply pick your top 3 goals, then answer the questions below. Keep writing even if you repeat your answers. The information below will help you feel clear, focused, and more motivated to achieve your goals.

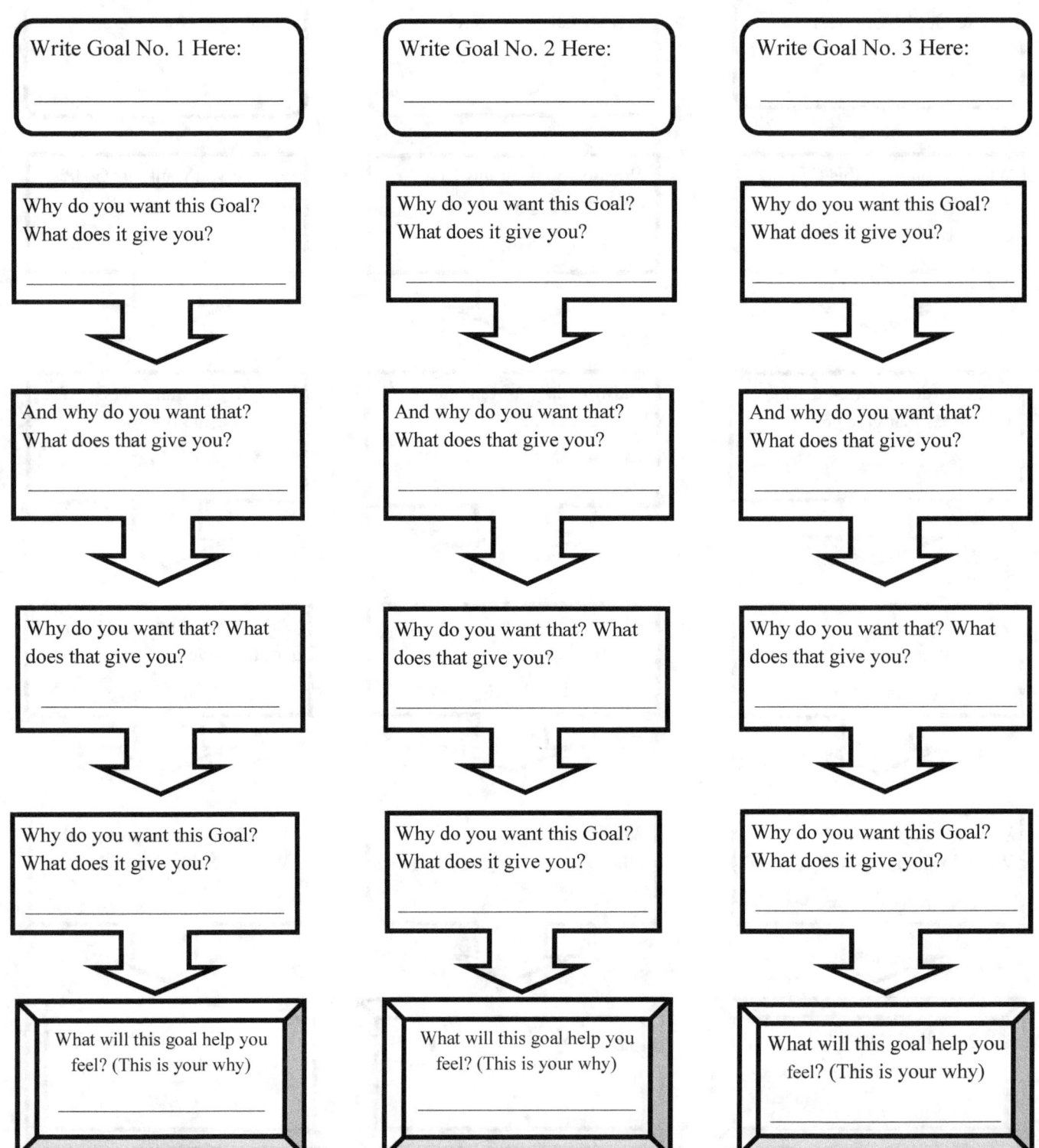

Write Goal No. 1 Here:
_____

Why do you want this Goal? What does it give you?
_____

And why do you want that? What does that give you?
_____

Why do you want that? What does that give you?
_____

Why do you want this Goal? What does it give you?
_____

What will this goal help you feel? (This is your why)
_____

Write Goal No. 2 Here:
_____

Why do you want this Goal? What does it give you?
_____

And why do you want that? What does that give you?
_____

Why do you want that? What does that give you?
_____

Why do you want this Goal? What does it give you?
_____

What will this goal help you feel? (This is your why)
_____

Write Goal No. 3 Here:
_____

Why do you want this Goal? What does it give you?
_____

And why do you want that? What does that give you?
_____

Why do you want that? What does that give you?
_____

Why do you want this Goal? What does it give you?
_____

What will this goal help you feel? (This is your why)
_____

Notes

Element IV:
Individual Development Action Plan

It's time to put some action to your words! How exciting!

The purpose of an Individual Development Action Plan is to help you reach your goals. An action plan is your personal strategic road map to your first desired destination. It helps you plan your actions, venture outside of your comfort zone, anticipate obstacles and create solutions to barriers, leverage your strengths, and identify resources and support for achieving your goals. The IDAP is your *who, what, when, where,* to your *why.*

It is important that you identify an accountability partner who will hold you accountable for reaching each goal and to your IDAP. Accountability partners are essential assets if you need additional encouragement, motivation, or someone to keep track of your progress. Your accountability partner should be someone you respect like a mentor, not someone whom you don't value as an authority figure.

For most of you, this workbook is the first time that you've experienced any form of coaching. If applied and used for its intended purpose, this process will be a transformation that includes renewing your mind and changing the way you view goals and success for the rest of your life. You'll be able to create a strategy to reach high levels of fulfillment. My ultimate desire is that you will teach yourself, and then teach someone else. It is my hope that you will join me in impacting the world, one person or group at a time!

This IDAP consists of five pages. I recommend that you thoroughly think each section through until completion. If you are motivated, ready for the challenge to overcome your environment, and live the life you desire, get started right away!

Timeframe to complete the Individual Development Action Plan: 2 weeks

What: My Personal Development Goals

Write your specific goals from the "Goals—Understanding the Why" worksheet and describe how/what you want to change or improve.

Ask yourself: What can I do differently/better that would make the greatest positive impact in my work? What development priorities will give me the greatest leverage in achieving my goals?

Goal 1

Goal 2

Goal 3

How: Action Steps I Will Take to Meet My Goals

Identify what you need to stop doing, start doing and keep doing. These short-term actions will contribute directly to your long-term goals.

1. Plan your actions.

Implement something every day. What situations, people or events signal that right now is the time to put new behaviors into action?	What new behavior will I try? Where will I push my comfort zone?
Every time I see the following situations:	…I will take the following action:
1. Example: Get overwhelmed	Take a break, create a to-do list, rank each task by importance and due date. Complete each task one at a time.
2.	
3.	

4.	
5.	

How: Action Steps I Will Take to Meet My Goals

2. Anticipate obstacles.

WATCH OUT: What barriers can I identify which might hinder me in pursuing my goals? How can I overcome these barriers?

Obstacle/Barrier	Solution
Example: Money for school	Apply for financial aid, scholarships, part-time job

3. Leverage strengths.

HINT: I have great strengths upon which to draw. Which of my strengths can I leverage to help me achieve my goals?

Strength	How will it help me achieve my goals?
Example: Computer Savvy	Create to-do lists, build charts, type homework, research schools

Who: Resources and Support for Achieving My Goals

How will I draw on my coach, peers, and others to track my progress, gather advice and feedback, and support for my progress?

Example: Share my progress and improvement areas with my accountability partner.

Who will I ask to support me? Who do I know who already possesses the competencies I want to build?

Example: Church member

With whom should I share my development plan?

Example: Mother

Accountability

When will I begin taking action to meet my goals?

Example: Today

When do I expect to see significant progress? (Milestone commitments)

How will I evaluate my progress?

How will I update my development strategy? When will I review my plan with those who helped me create it?

How will I leverage what I learn?

Acknowledgement

What will be the impact of meeting my goals on me and my career?

How will I benefit from the changes/improvements I have identified?

How will I celebrate when I meet my goals?

Goals (SMART)	Time frame	Outcome	Completed Date

Notes

Resumes

An important aspect of career planning is developing or updating your resume. Resumes are documents that provide potential employers with a detailed overview of your professional work history, to include relevant skills, and education and training. The purpose of resumes is to not get you the job, but to secure interviews.

Your resume is the first impression potential employers may have of you. Therefore, you want to paint a professional, organized, and accurate picture of who you are and your performance in the workplace. You should update your resume each time you obtain a new job or position. Look at the tables below to learn or review how to write an effective resume.

What information should be in a resume?	
• Your Contact Information	• Work or Volunteer Experience
• Objective or Profile	• Education & Professional Training
• Skills	• Professional Associations

If you are familiar with resumes, notice that I did not include a row for "References". Employers are aware that if they request references, you will provide them. Save space on your resume by only including pertinent information. Put yourself in the employer's shoes. The next two tables will provide you with characteristics of a successful resume and a basic resume checklist.

Characteristics of A Successful Resume	
• Focuses on skills. Uses action words to define the responsibilities of your job-related experience.	• Produced on a computer.
• Easy to read and understand.	• Data presented in chronological order.
• One page, or at most 2 pages long, with the exception of federal resumes.	• Formal style.
• Language is grammatically correct. Spelling has been checked.	• Must always be 100% truthful.

Basic Resume Checklist	
• Neat, clean, and professional looking.	• Quantify your results whenever you can.
• Margins at sides and bottom.	• Format—chronological or combined.
• Important titles should be emphasized. No more than 2 different font sizes.	• Information is logically recorded.
• Bullet points when possible for accomplishments.	• Use action verbs for accomplishments and results.

Often times, we don't keep track of our daily responsibilities that we perform on the job. It will be helpful to visit your current or previous employer's website, search for your position, and use the duties and responsibilities applicable to you. If the employer does not have a website, simply search the internet for the position you held, even if the position is that of another company, and use parts of the description that you performed. Don't forget to quantify the description to your accomplishments during your work period,

On the next two pages, you will find sample resume templates for both high school students and career professionals. Pay close attention to the differences of each section. I have also included a list of resume action verbs and a resume planning worksheet for your use.

SAMPLE HIGH SCHOOL TEMPLATE

JOHN SMITH

123 Farms Village Road   (860) 423-5731

Simsbury, CT 06070   jsmith@yahoo.com

Objective   The Objective is a brief statement which expresses a goal for employment or college. It tells the reader what you want to do. Begin your objective with "To…" For example: "To attend a four-year college and obtain a business degree"

Education   Simsbury High School   Simsbury, CT

Honors/Awards

High School Honor Roll   00/0000
National Honor Society   00/0000
Simsbury Scholar   00/0000

Extracurricular

Varsity Basketball   00/0000—00/0000

SHS Connect Leader   00/0000—00/0000
Freshman Band   00/0000—00/0000

Employment

Cashier   00/0000– Present

Little City Pizza, City, State

- Process customer payments by cash, credit, and debit cards

- Take to go and dine in orders by phone and in-person

- Coordinate with hostess, floor, and kitchen staff regarding special customer requests

Community Service/Volunteer Experience

Church Acolyte   00/0000—00/0000

Relay for Life participant   00/0000—00/0000

SAMPLE PROFESSIONAL TEMPLATE

John W. Smith

Washington, DC

Phone: (555) 555-5555 E-mail: johnwsmith@yahoo.com

ADMINISTRATIVE ASSISTANT

Meticulous and dedicated administrative professional with eight years of experience in customer service, documentation, records management, and process improvement. Possesses advanced knowledge in data entry, customer confidentiality, and inventory management. Applies strong solution based approach to conflict resolution and continual organization improvement.

Core Competencies

· Records Management	· Quality Improvement	· Team Building
· Customer Service	· Communication	· Critical Thinking
· Organization	· Automated Data Entry	· Computer Savvy
· Staff Training & Development	· Regulatory Compliance	· Documentation

Experience

Administrative Assistant   00/0000—00/0000

Roosevelt, Inc. – Boston, MA

- Coordinated and administered 245 graduation exams in accordance with policies and procedures established by exam agencies
- Registered approximately 100 qualified students to vote
- Published 5-7 articles in local community newspaper pertaining to classroom activities involving students and parents

Your Position Title   00/0000—00/0000

Roosevelt, Inc. – Boston, MA

- Previous duties and responsibility 1
- Previous duties and responsibility 2
- Previous duties and responsibility 3

Education

Such and such certification, course 1-8

Valley Village School of Such and Such, 2010

BS, Mathematics

Florida State College, Miami Florida, 2009

Resume Action Verbs

Management/Leadership Skills						
Administered	Analyzed	Appointed	Approved	Assigned	Attained	Authorized
Chaired	Consolidated	Contracted	Controlled	Coordinated	Delegated	Developed
Directed	Eliminated	Enforced	Enhanced	Established	Generated	Hired
Improved	Inspected	Led	Managed	Motivated	Organized	Planned

Communication / People Skills						
Addressed	Advertised	Arbitrated	Arranged	Articulated	Authored	Classified
Collaborated	Communicated	Composed	Condensed	Consulted	Contacted	Defined
Described	Discussed	Drafted	Edited	Explained	Formulated	Incorporated
Influenced	Interviewed	Joined	Lectured	Listened	Marketed	Promoted

Research Skills						
Clarified	Collected	Compared	Conducted	Critiqued	Detected	Determined
Diagnosed	Examined	Explored	Extracted	Formulated	Gathered	Identified
Interpreted	Invented	Investigated	Located	Measured	Organized	Researched
Searched	Solved	Summarized	Surveyed	Systematized	Tested	

Others						
Adapted	Advocated	Aided	Answered	Arranged	Assessed	Assisted
Cared for	Coached	Cooperated	Contributed	Encouraged	Approved	Charted
Collected	Filed	Logged	Maintained	Ordered	Restored	Resolved
Simplified	Spearheaded	Succeeded	Surpassed	Transformed	Updated	Verified

RESUME PLANNING WORKSHEET

<u>Personal Information</u>

Full Name _____ Email _____

Address _____ City, State, Zip _____

Phone _____

Objective

While most resumes do not require this section, it can be helpful to put down your objective as a reminder of your job goal. (Ex. To work full time as a Machine Operator. OR To utilize 10 years of experience in Customer Service.

_____

Work History (reverse chronological order)

Work history is a list of the places you have worked and what duties you had on the job. This section starts with your most recent job and ends with your least recent.

Example:

Courier – Messages-R-Us, Inc.

Manchester, NY –May 2014—May 2015

- Logged 7,000 miles
- Ensured accurate records for miles driven and deliveries
- Reported any and all issues to supervisor and made suggestions for improvement

Job Title _____

Company Name _____ Start date (month and year) _____

City, State _____ End date (month and year) _____

Job duties, skills, responsibilities (list at least 4)

_____

_____

_____

_____

Job Title _____

Company Name _____ Start date (month and year) _____

City, State _____ Start date (month and year) _____

Job duties, skills, responsibilities (list at least 4)

_____

_____

_____

_____

Volunteer Experience

Organization Name _____

Job Title _____ Start date (month and year) _____

City, State _____ End date (month and year) _____

Job duties, skills, responsibilities

_____

_____

_____

Organization Name _____

Job Title _____ Start date (month and year) _____

City, State _____ End date (month and year) _____

Job duties, skills, responsibilities

_____

_____

_____

Education

Degree/Certification/Diploma obtained/pursuing _____

School Name _____

City, State _____

Special activities or classes involved in _____

Degree/Certification/Diploma obtained/pursuing _____

School Name _____

City, State _____

Special activities or classes involved in _____

_____

Notes

Part II: Basic Entrepreneurship

The Nature of Being an Entrepreneur

Researching & Planning the business

Choosing a Partner

Understanding Part Two: Entrepreneurship

Part two is a brief discussion into entrepreneurship. It provides entry level understanding the nature of being an entrepreneur, business plans, and the legality of starting a business. The world of entrepreneurship is too broad to cover all of the aspects in this workbook. However, you may visit www.kaynorth.com and enroll in 14 Week Passion Ignited or 2 Week Next Level Unlocked.

Entrepreneurship is an exciting journey and lifestyle. Did you notice that? It's a lifestyle. Once you dive into entrepreneurship, it's hard to go back to traditional work. In this section of the workbook, we'll discuss the nature of being an entrepreneur, research and planning the business, and choosing a business partner. We cannot got into as much detail as needed, however, 14 Week Passion Ignited will answer all of your questions.

The Nature of Being an Entrepreneur

An entrepreneur must be both a leader and a manager. Starting a new business requires you to be the visionary, research & development, marketing and sales, the supervisor and the employee, finance, logistics, everything, unless you are able to hire an expert of each area. Some of the characteristics and traits needed will be learned and developed as you go. Below is a chart of characteristics and traits of a successful entrepreneur.

Characteristics and Traits of Entrepreneurs	
Determination	Risk taker
Creative	Free-spirited
Confidence	Craves learning
Passionate	Highly adaptable
Money management	Interpersonal
Resilience	Vision & intuitive

Majority of people who desire to be an entrepreneur, do so because they want to be in control of their time and freedom and want more money. Here is a list of advantages and disadvantages of entrepreneurship. Note that the listed advantages and disadvantages may or may not be an advantage or disadvantage for you depending on your likes and dislikes, and strengths and weaknesses.

Advantages	Disadvantages
Control	Administration
Excitement	Failed ideas
Flexibility	Competition
Freedom	Loneliness
Rational Salary	No regular salary
Networking	Work schedule
Filling a need	
Learning experiences	

Researching and Planning the Business

Business Plan

Business plans are documents used for planning out specific details about your business. The primary purpose of a business plan is to define what the business is or what it intends to be over time. It is important to understand that plans will change!

Framework of a Business Plan
• Typically 15-20 pages
• Three major sections
• Seven sub components
• Appendix (pictures, samples, etc.)

Major Sections	Sub-Components
Business Concept	Executive Summary
Marketplace Strategy	Description of business (mission statement, objective, goals)
Financial Plan	Market Strategies
	Competition Analysis
	Product & Services
	Operations & Management
	Financial Analysis

On the next page, you'll find seven easy steps to complete a simple business plan.

Business Plan in Seven Steps

1. Start with a vision.

What does it look like? Who's there? What colors do you see? What is the vibe? Is there music? What are the people doing? Are there decorations? Do you have a staff? Do you see money? How many people? Is there food? Are there tables? Is there an unhappy person? How are lives affected?

Create a picture of your overall vision and put it on paper, preferably in a designated notebook. If you have a difficult time putting your thoughts into words, try drawing on paper or speaking into a recorder. Once you draw or speak your vision, then write what you have drawn or spoke. It is imperative that the vision is written plainly on paper.

2. Break the vision down into smaller details.

Breaking down each section of your overall vision into smaller details allows you to organize ideas for creation, inventory, and cost. For instance, when you see the decorations in your vision, are there centerpieces, confetti, and banners? For the centerpiece, your materials would include silk flowers, a glue gun, glue sticks, floral foam, or custom-designed by a professional. If you visualize your staff or team, how many people are there, are they male or female, how many male or females, what color are they wearing, are they wearing the same t-shirt design, are they paid staff or volunteers, and how are they behaving? Not only does sectioning your vision into smaller portions help you focus on the details, it also enables you to create a to-do list, delegate tasks to helpers, create a budget, and seek resources.

3. Identify your target audience.

Who is your customer? What does your customer look like? What does he/she need? Where does he/she shop? Do they use social media? What do they do or visit for fun? How will you reach your customers?

Identifying your target market/audience is a task that must be thought out thoroughly and realistically. Your product/service could possibly target everyone, but not realistically. The best way to identify your customer is by creating avatars. From your vision, think about the questions above. Use Google to find an image of a person or clipart that will serve as one of your customer. Give her/him a profile, including name, age, income, brief background, and their need. As many different customers you imagine from your vision, create an equal number of avatars with all differing profiles. Then, list the marketing methods best for reaching each avatar, i.e., social media, newspaper, brochures. Doing this identifies your target customer and creates your marketing strategy.

4. Set value.

How much are customers willing to pay? How does your product/service compare to existing products/services? What is your advantage? Does your product/service create an effect? Determining the value of your product/service can be tricky as we instinctively value our own creations higher than anyone else. However, as women, we tend to undervalue our worth. The value of a product/service is determined by several factors, such as: quality, supply and demand, accessibility competitor pricing, location, uniqueness, and perception. There is no short cut to determine pricing. This will require homework by researching the target area, nearby competitors as well as online, customer perception via surveys or testing, and creating your advantage.

The value of your product/service should be conveyed in your message to your target and fit your vision.

By this point, you should know the product/service you're providing, material budget, target audience, comparison to competitors, the effect of products/service, marketing strategy, and pricing. All of these aspects have a role in the message you must convey. Your message must be concise, meaningful, and powerful. It becomes your brand!

5. Overcome Fear

There are two common obstacles that many of us will face on this journey—fear and finances. We're going to discuss the most crippling obstacle, fear. Fear of the unknown is the number one paralysis of potentially great people. The perception of failure in venturing outside of your comfort zone is an illusion that causes you to become stationary or ride the hamster wheel. However, if you replace the energy you give to the perception of failing with a perception of adventure, fear changes to excitement! You should be excited to venture into unknown territories. The only options you'll face once we take the first step are to be conquerors or learners. You can never fail! You can only conquer or learn and then conquer! That's a cycle worth repeating—"Either I conquer the first time, or I learn from a mistake, go back, and conquer!"

6. Collaboration/ Partnership

Collaborating with other business leaders provide great benefits financially and supportively. No one was created to live or work alone. We all have something that another person needs. Collaborating or partnering with others can help strengthen weak areas, broaden insight, and provide a variety of products, services, or resources to your target audience. When considering joining other business leaders, it is imperative that each party establishes a mutual understanding and agreement of boundaries, what is being offered, shared expenses, and the message and appearance that is being conveyed prior to any performance of business activities. Well-meshed collaboration should be a win-win for all parties involved, especially the audience.

7. Ready, Set, Go!

This may be new for you as you move towards your vision. At this point, you have the essential information of a basic business plan. All you have to do is put all of your information together, pick a date, and launch! Even if you move at a snail's pace, you are still moving. In the beginning, don't be discouraged by a low turnout. Low turnouts present great opportunities to make lasting impressions and build relationships with those who do participate. Word of mouth spreads quickly, and you want those words to be positive. However, if some words are negative, use those to your advantage by making adjustments and asking customers/ clients for feedback. Doing so sends a clear message that you care about your product/service, brand, and the experience of your audience.

Legal Structures

While drafting your business plan, it is important to identify which legal structure will work for your business. The most common types of legal structure for small businesses are sole proprietorship, limited liability company, and partnership. Use Google to research each legal structure to identify which will work best for you.

	Partnership	Limited Partnership	Limited Liability Company (LLC)	Sole Proprietorship
What it is	A business whose gains and losses are passed to individual partners.	A partnership with many of the liability protections of a corporation.	A cross between a corporation and a partnership.	A business that operates under the endorsement of an individual.
Ownership	Owned by two or more partners	Owned b a general partner who controls the business and limited partners who have no active role.	Owned by "members" similar to shareholders, may be managed by a member or by a manager.	Owned by a person.
Taxes	Taxes are passed through to the partners.	Taxes are passed through to the partners.	May be taxed as a pass-through entity or as a tax-paying association.	Owner pays income tax and 15.3% self employment tax.

State Requirements	Federal Requirements
Business Name (Entity) Reservation	Employer Identification Number
Certificate of Formation	
Business License & Permits	
State Tax Registration	

Partnerships

Many entrepreneurs decide to partner with another person and go into business. A partnership is a single business where two or more people share ownership. Each partner contributes to all aspects of the business, including money, property, labor, or skill. In return, each partner shares in the profits and losses of the business. Below is a list of pros and cons of partnerships.

Pros	Cons
Easy and inexpensive business structure	Management issues
Shared financial commitment	Disagreements among partners
Complementary skills	Lack of an exit strategy
More ideas	Transferability
Simplified taxes	Lacking a written and signed partnership agreement
	Subpar skills

While there are many advantages to partnerships, it is important to be wise in choosing a partner. See potential ways to choose a evaluate a potential business partner.

Choosing a Partner: Qualifications
Evaluate qualifications without emotions
Assess communication styles
Do a background check (criminal, reputation, and standing with the community)
Have a plan for resolving conflict
Do a trial run
Matching values, but different skills/abilities
Financially stable
Strong commitment level
Handles pressure, obstacles, & challenges well
An old friend or respected family member does not mean a good business partner!

Partnership Agreement

 You will find that in business, paperwork is extremely important. It is critically imperative when conducting business with another party. Documentation detailing the scope of business, including the who, when, what, where, and how, should be drafted, mutually agreed upon, and signed by all persons involved prior to any business activities are performed. Doing so will save time, energy, and money. The same conduct must be performed in partnership agreements. The information below details the five clauses that every partnership should include.

Five Clauses Every Partnership Agreement Should Have
Decision-making
Capital contribution
Salaries / distribution
Death / disability
Dissolution

This concludes the entrepreneur section. If you would like more in-depth training, again, you may contact me to enroll in entrepreneurial coaching.

Notes

Part III:

Internal & External Changes

Mindset

Time Management

Friends: Changing Your Circle

Understanding Part III: Changes

Part three covers the necessary internal and external changes that must be made on your journey. These changes may take place in your mindset, time managing skills, and in your association of friends and family members.

You will find a learning chart, an activity, and a sample list to assist in furthering your learning and development over time. There is no time frame to complete assignments. Take your time to allow the material to absorb in your mind, recognize situations as they are presented, and implement the necessary changes as you go.

Necessary Internal & External Changes

Now that you've performed the research required for career exploration, aligned SMART goals, determined your *why*, and completed your Individual Development Action Plan, it is important that you realize there will be necessary internal and external changes that must be made to yourself and your immediate environment. "WHY?" you ask? Because you cannot reach significant levels of success by staying the same. For the remainder of the book, we'll discuss mindset, time management, and friends. Each area will impact stages of your journey to success.

Mindset

Question: are people born smart? Let's consider some noteworthy people who made history. Beethoven's teacher called him a hopeless composer. He wrote five of his greatest symphonies while deaf. Einstein's teacher said he was 'academically subnormal'. Michael Jordan's coach said he wasn't more talented than other people. Walt Disney was told that he lacked 'creative imagination'. Each example illustrates great people who had nay-sayers and were thought to be subpar. Well, would you look at them now! Who got the last laugh?! What made the difference?

Mindset!

According to scholars, there are two types of mindsets: growth and fixed. The chart below differentiates fixed mindset from growth mindset. Study the chart. Identify your current mindset. If you have traits of fixed mindset, think of ways that you can transform that area of your mind to the growth mindset. It is doable. After all, our great people in history shows us that we can achieve anything!

Fixed Mindset		Growth Mindset
• Innate • Unchanging	**SKILLS**	• Result of hard work • Can always improve
• Something to avoid • Will reveal lack of skill • Overwhelm	**CHALLENGES**	• Embrace • Opportunity to change • Calls for perseverance
• Not necessary • Linked to being not good enough	**EFFORT**	• Essential • Leads to mastery
• Produces defensiveness • Personalized	**FEEDBACK**	• Useful and positive • Welcomed • Identify areas to improve
• Blame others, not my fault • Easily discouraging	**SETBACKS**	• Opportunities to learn form • Focus on making changes

Time Management

Let's start this section off with an activity that is common in the coaching profession. Participate by following the directions before moving on. We all like money, so the name of this game is Time Value of Money. I am super rich, and I've decided to give you $86,400! That's right, eighty six thousand four hundred dollars! You must spend it all within 24 hours. You cannot save or invest any of it. How would you spend it? Be very specific. Use a calculator if necessary. Don't cheat!

_____

_____

_____

_____

_____.

_____

_____

Ok, the object of this game is to see how you would spend your money. We've all heard the cliché, "time is money". The way you spend your money is a direct reflection of how you would spend your money. The $86,400 represents the number of seconds in time that we all have in each day. Take a look at the bulk of where you spent your money. Then convert the money into seconds, which equates to the amount of time you would spend in that area. How does where you spend your money rank in priority to how you would spend your time? For instance, if the largest portion of your money would go to wardrobe and the next largest is to education, this correlates to you would spend more time on your wardrobe than your education. In this case, your priorities need adjustment.

What you accomplish during a 24-hour period depends on your own motivation, your energy, your skills and abilities, and other resources. Since there are always demands on your time, it may be helpful to think about what you will do with your time and consider some strategies for more effective time management. Time management is not a way to make you work harder and longer, but a means to help you work smarter to accomplish your work more easily and rapidly.

Obstacles to Effective Time Management

In order to manage your time more effectively, we must be aware of obstacles that prevent us from managing our time

- **Unclear Objectives**: It's hard to hit a target with your eyes closed, and it's just as hard to accomplish something when you aren't exactly clear about what you want to achieve.

- **Disorganization**: It's easy to see when your desk is too messy, but sometimes you have to step back and ask yourself if you are taking an organized approach in completing all of your tasks.

- **Inability to say "No"**: We all want to be as helpful as we can when others need us, but this can mean taking time away from other priorities to do something we may not have planned.

- **Interruptions**: We all like to visit with others, talk on the phone, engage on social media, but conversations at inappropriate times can cost us time when we have to stop what we are doing and redirect ourselves from our plans.

- **Periods of inactivity**: Making use of down time can have positive effect on our efforts.

- **Too many things at once**

- **Stress and fatigue**

- **All work and no play**

Most of the above mentioned time wasters are distractions. So what can we do? Recognize that obstacles exist, identify them, and employ strategies to overcome the distractions. The most successful way to overcome obstacles is to **prioritize** by making a To Do List. Some tasks can be delegated or deleted.

Do—Determine from the list of things you think are most important to accomplish, and are things you should do yourself.

Delegate—Ask a reliable friend/family member/co-worker to help you with tasks that are within their capacity.

Delay—until another time. Some things can wait.

Delete—As an effective individual, you must know when to concentrate on the important and eliminate the rest.

When prioritizing, first address the urgent, then accomplish what you can early, and attach deadlines to things you delay.

Must Do Today	Must Be Done By_____	Upcoming Due Dates

Friends: Changing Your Circle

"Started from the bottom, now we here. Started from the bottom, now the whole team here."

Maybe you've heard this song by Drake. It has a catchy beat, and I actually like it! However, realistically, there are only a hand full of people who actually have the same friends from childhood as they do when they reach their desired level of success.

Why?

Because as your life takes on the direction of your desired destination and your mindset begins to transform, the things you once had in common with your circle of friends will change. If those friends aren't traveling on a journey to success along with you, you will simply outgrow them. You will naturally gravitate to people who are working hard with purpose, who can share an understanding of the everyday struggle and sacrifice that you endure.

Growing into who you want to be may cause strains in certain relationships among family and friends. Some people have become used to being able to call on you whenever they need you, and you drop everything to help. However, once you have a sense of direction for your life and begin working towards it, your time must be managed effectively. While your intentions will be sincere, you will have to learn to say no to things that pose as a distraction to your priority list. Saying no will not always be welcomed, thus drawing backlash from those who do not understand this new you.

Friends may be used to meeting you for drinks or going to a party. However, the new you who now has goals to work towards, will have to sacrifice some friend outings to do homework or attend a development workshop. Some friends will understand; others won't. You will hear backlash such as, "oh, you're too good for us now." Don't worry, it comes with the territory. Keep working towards your direction.

On the other hand, you may be able to effectively communicate the necessary sacrifices you must make to friends and family beforehand to make your transition smooth and build a foundation of understanding. Those who will accept the growing you will be supporters. Those who won't accept the growing you, will not support you. Often times, your growth will make those who won't support you uncomfortable because your growth takes away their excuses to not grow.

Be prepared to lose some people along your journey. The ones you lose will be replaced with ones of better quality.

Notes

Closing Remarks

You are now equipped with a strategy for your direction and have an understanding of the necessary internal and external changes to your environment that must be made on your journey to success. I recommend that you take your time, commit to your journey, and most importantly, KEEP GOING!

For those of you who are entrepreneurs at heart, you may contact me to enroll in my entrepreneur program. We will explore every aspect of the lifestyle, leaving no rock uncovered. After the 14 week course, you will equipped with priceless knowledge to walk into the entrepreneurial adventure.

It is my prayer that you maximize your potential at each stage of your journey. I would love to hear from you. You may contact me via the following methods:

www.facebook.com/coachkaynorth | info@kaynorth.com | www.kaynorth.com.

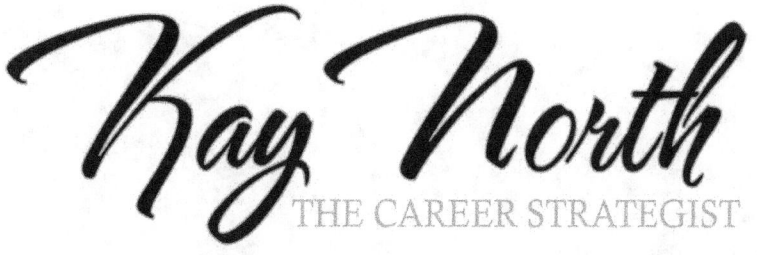